TITANIC

Robin Johnson

CRABTREE
Publishing Company
www.crabtreebooks.com

Crabtree Publishing Company

www.crabtreebooks.com

Author: Robin Johnson
Publishing plan research and development:
  Sean Charlebois, Reagan Miller
  Crabtree Publishing Company
Project coordinator: Kathy Middleton
Photo research: Steve White-Thomson
Editor: Sonya Newland
Proofreader: Crystal Sikkens
Design: Tim Mayer (Mayer Media)
Cover design: Ken Wright
**Production coordinator and prepress
  technician:** Ken Wright
Print coordinator: Katherine Berti

Produced for Crabtree Publishing by
White-Thomson Publishing

Reading levels determined by
Publishing Solutions Group.
Content level: R
Readability level: L

Photographs:
Alamy: Moviestore Collection Ltd: pp. 24,
  30–31
Bridgeman Art Library: © Look and Learn:
  front cover
Corbis: p. 36; Hulton-Deutsch Collection:
  pp. 3, 8–9; Heritage Images: p. 18;
  National Geographic Society: pp. 32–33,
  35, 44–45; Bettmann: pp. 21, 37
Getty Images: pp. 14, 40; De Agostini:
  pp. 4–5
Library of Congress: pp. 25, 38, 39, 41
Mary Evans Picture Library: Onslow
  Auctions Ltd: pp. 12, 16–17, 23; Illustrated
  London News Ltd: pp. 20, 27
NOAA: IFE/URI: pp. 42–43, 43
Shutterstock: back cover, icon
Topfoto.co.uk: pp. 13, 22, 31
Wikimedia: pp. 6, 7, 10, 11, 15, 26–27,
  28–29, 34

Library and Archives Canada Cataloguing in Publication

CIP available at Library and Archives Canada

Library of Congress Cataloging-in-Publication Data

Johnson, Robin (Robin R.)
Titanic / Robin Johnson.
   p. cm. -- (Crabtree chrome)
   Includes index.
   Audience: Ages 11-14.
   ISBN 978-0-7787-7929-2 (reinforced library binding) --
ISBN 978-0-7787-7938-4 (pbk.) -- ISBN 978-1-4271-7859-6
(electronic .pdf) -- ISBN 978-1-4271-7974-6 (electronic .html)
   1. Titanic (Steamship)--Juvenile literature. 2. Shipwrecks--
North Atlantic Ocean--Juvenile literature. I. Title.
   G530.T6J64 2012
   910.9163'4--dc22
                                               2012032206

Crabtree Publishing Company

Printed in Canada/102012/MA20120817

www.crabtreebooks.com   1-800-387-7650

Published in Canada
Crabtree Publishing
616 Welland Ave.
St. Catharines, ON
L2M 5V6

Published in the United States
Crabtree Publishing
PMB 59051
350 Fifth Avenue, 59th Floor
New York, New York 10118

Published in the United Kingdom
Crabtree Publishing
Maritime House
Basin Road North, Hove
BN41 1WR

Published in Australia
Crabtree Publishing
3 Charles Street
Coburg North
VIC 3058

Contents

Ship of Dreams

Ocean Liner

The *Titanic* was called the "ship of dreams."
It was a huge **ocean liner** built in 1912.
The *Titanic* was the biggest and best ship
in the world. Sadly, the ship of dreams
became a nightmare for all on board.

▼ *The* Titanic *was a huge ship.*
It was as long as three football fields.

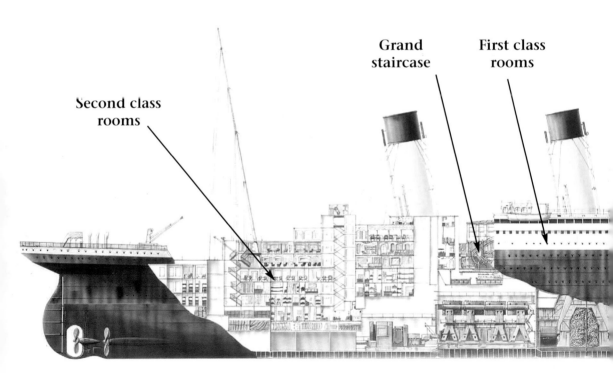

Second class rooms

Grand staircase

First class rooms

882 feet (269 meters)

Bigger is Better

The word "titanic" means huge or powerful. The *Titanic* was both of those things. It held more than 3,500 people. It had two strong engines and could travel fast for such a big ship.

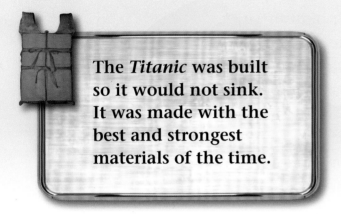

The *Titanic* was built so it would not sink. It was made with the best and strongest materials of the time.

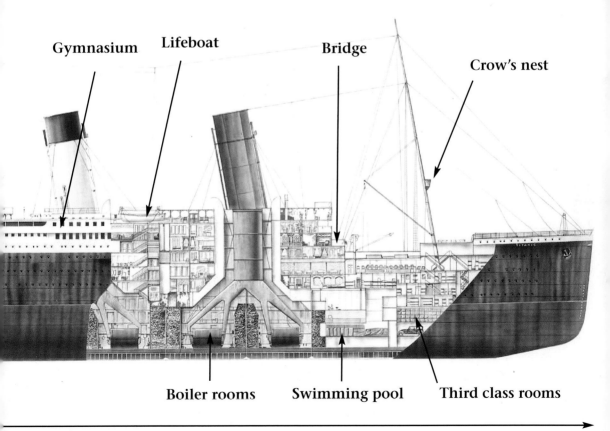

Gymnasium   Lifeboat   Bridge   Crow's nest

Boiler rooms   Swimming pool   Third class rooms

ocean liner: a large passenger ship with many comforts

Luxury Liner

The *Titanic* was a **luxury** ship. Every room on board seemed bigger and nicer than the last. There were grand rooms for sleeping, eating, or relaxing. There was even a swimming pool on board!

▲ *Passengers in first class could eat in a French café.*

▲ *First class on the* Titanic *had all the comforts of home.*

Comfort Levels

The *Titanic* had different levels. First class was on the upper level. This was the finest part of the *Titanic*. Second class and third class were the lower parts of the ship. These areas had fewer luxuries but were still very nice.

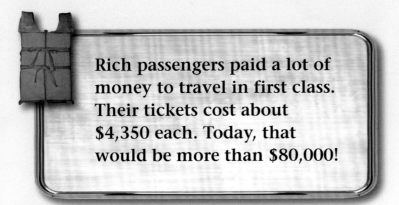

Rich passengers paid a lot of money to travel in first class. Their tickets cost about $4,350 each. Today, that would be more than $80,000!

 luxury: something fine or special that costs a lot of money

The Titanic Sails

Maiden Voyage

The *Titanic* was ready to sail for New York on April 10, 1912. It was the great ship's **maiden voyage**. Excitement was in the air. Crowds came to watch the lucky men, women, and children board the *Titanic* for its first trip.

▼ *The* Titanic *set sail at noon from Southampton, England.*

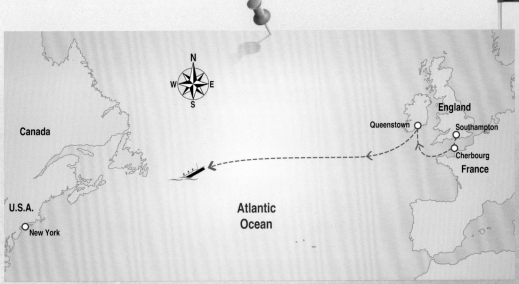

Welcome Aboard!

The ship's band played lively music to welcome passengers. People waved and threw flowers as the ship began to sail. The sky was clear and the waters were calm. It was going to be a good trip.

▲ *This map shows the planned route of the* Titanic. *It would take about a week to reach New York City.*

maiden voyage: a ship's first trip

All Aboard

More than 1,300 passengers boarded the *Titanic* that day. They came from all walks of life. Some people were rich and famous. They were used to the finer things in life. They found them in first class on the *Titanic*.

▲ *The gym in first class had exercise bikes and a rowing machine.*

▲ *The Goodwins were one of the poor immigrant families on board the* Titanic.

Second and Third

Most people were in second class or third class. Some were traveling for work. Others were on vacation. Many people in second class and third class were **immigrants**. They were moving to America for a better life.

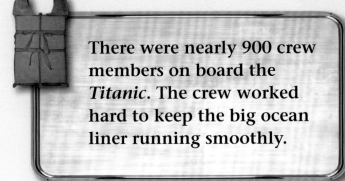

There were nearly 900 crew members on board the *Titanic*. The crew worked hard to keep the big ocean liner running smoothly.

 immigrants: people who go to live in a new country

Life on Board

During the day, passengers in first class **strolled** on the upper decks of the ship. They played sports and swam in the ship's pool. At night, people dressed up and ate fine meals like lobster and duck. Then they slept in grand bedrooms.

▼ *People in second class strolled or sat on their own deck.*

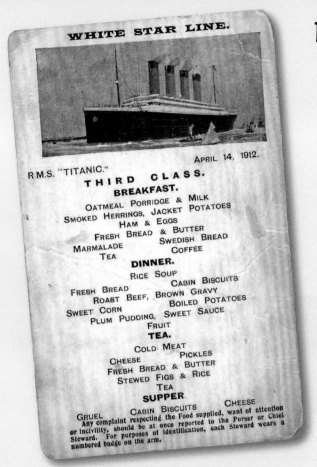

 Passengers in third class got four simple but tasty meals each day.

Lower Classes

Second class was almost as good as first class. People in second class ate tasty meals and slept in lovely rooms in the middle part of the ship. Passengers in third class stayed in nice cabins in the bottom part of the ship.

"I enjoyed myself as if I were on a summer palace by the seashore."

Archibald Gracie, a passenger in first class

strolled: walked slowly for pleasure

Iceberg!

Danger

The *Titanic* sped through the ocean for four days. On April 14, Captain Smith got radio warnings. There were deadly **icebergs** in the area. The captain changed the course of the ship. He did not slow down, though.

▲ *This photograph shows chunks of ice in the place where the* Titanic *sank.*

◀ *Captain Smith wanted to surprise the world by arriving in New York earlier than planned.*

Full Steam Ahead!

Captain Smith wanted to show the world just what the mighty *Titanic* could do. He told his crew to go faster and faster. The ship was going so fast that it would be hard to stop or steer it around an iceberg.

> **"Shut up! Shut up! I am busy."**
>
> Crewman John Phillips, answering a final radio warning about icebergs near the *Titanic*

 icebergs: mountains of ice that float in the ocean

Look Out!

At 11:40 p.m., a lookout saw an iceberg right in front of the ship! He rang the alarm bell three times to alert the captain and crew. Then the lookout phoned the **bridge**. He yelled, "Iceberg, right ahead!"

Crow's nest

Bridge

ICEBERG!

Too Late

A member of the crew was steering the ship. He turned the wheel quickly as far as it would go. It was too late. Seconds later, the *Titanic* hit the iceberg.

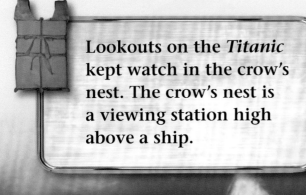

Lookouts on the *Titanic* kept watch in the crow's nest. The crow's nest is a viewing station high above a ship.

▼ *The lookout did not see the iceberg in front of the ship until it was too late.*

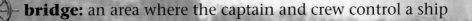

bridge: an area where the captain and crew control a ship

Crash!

The *Titanic* **collided** with the huge iceberg.
The ship scraped slowly along the ice. The
iceberg made a long hole in the side of the
ship. Chunks of ice landed on the deck.
Then the *Titanic* came to a stop.

Too Much Water

The captain rushed to check the damage. He saw water pouring into the bottom of the ship. There was too much water to hold. Soon the rest of the ship would fill with water. The captain could not save the *Titanic*.

"It was as though we went over about a thousand marbles."

Titanic passenger Ella White, describing the crash

◀ *The* Titanic *collided with a huge, hard iceberg.*

collided: crashed into another object

Sinking Ship

The captain knew the *Titanic* would sink quickly. There were so many men, women, and children on board. They had to be saved! The captain told his crew to radio for help right away.

▲ *Using radios to send messages from ships was a new idea at the time of the* Titanic.

Calling for Help

The crew called for any nearby ships to come and help the *Titanic*. A ship named *Carpathia* answered the call. It was coming to save them! The *Carpathia* was quite far away, though. Would it get there in time?

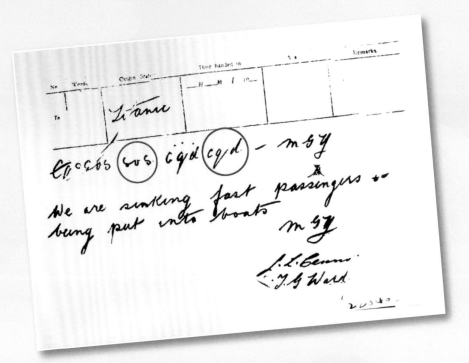

▲ *The last radio message from the* Titanic *read,*
"We are sinking fast passengers being put into boats."

The crew sent **distress signals** on the ship's radios. The crew used the codes "CQD" and "SOS." These codes meant the *Titanic* was in danger.

 distress signals: radio signals that mean a ship is in danger

The Bad News

The captain and crew told people the bad news. The *Titanic* was sinking. People had to **abandon** the ship or they would die. The crew told passengers to dress warmly and put on their life jackets.

▲ *Passengers had walked past the lifeboats for days. Now it was time to use the boats.*

Not True!

Many people did not believe they were in danger. They kept eating and dancing. Some people went back to sleep. Soon, water inside the *Titanic* began to rise. Then people knew the big ship was in big trouble.

▲ *This mother read a book to her child as the* Titanic *was sinking.*

"It will take more than an iceberg to get *me* out of bed."

A passenger on the *Titanic*, who stayed in bed while the ship sank

 abandon: to leave a place and never go back to it

Abandon Ship!

Who Goes First?

The crew began to help passengers get into lifeboats. There was only enough room for about half the people on board, though. The captain told his crew to put women and children into the lifeboats first.

▲ *Many women and children survived in the* Titanic's *lifeboats.*

◀ *Isidor Straus sat with his wife on the deck until a huge wave washed them away.*

No Thanks!

Some women would not leave the sinking ship. They thought that the **sturdy** *Titanic* was safer than the little lifeboats. Many people did not speak English. They did not know what was going on. Other women would not leave their men behind.

> "We have lived together for many years. Where you go, I go."
>
> Ida Straus, who climbed out of a lifeboat to stay with her husband, Isidor

sturdy: solid and strong

Fighting for Their Lives

Some men began to panic. They wanted to get off the sinking ship. The men fought for a place in the lifeboats. They shoved and hit one another. Some rich men tried to buy their way on to the lifeboats.

▲ *Some crew members went in the lifeboats to help row.*

▶ *Men kissed their wives and children goodbye, and helped them climb into the lifeboats.*

Noble Men

Other men were **noble** and brave. They put their wives and children safely into the lifeboats. Some men told their families they would meet in New York, to try to reassure them as they got in the boat.

> **"I'll see you in New York!"**
>
> Thomas Brown, waving to his wife and daughter as they boarded a lifeboat. He was never seen again.

 noble: being good and brave by helping others rather than yourself

Jumping Ship

Some bold people jumped off the sinking ship. They put on life jackets if they had them, then said a prayer and took the plunge. A few lucky jumpers were picked up by lifeboats. Most were not so lucky.

▼ *Some people jumped from the* Titanic *into the icy water below.*

Icy Waters

Most people died of **hypothermia** in the icy water. The water in the ocean was below freezing that night. No one could last for long in water so cold.

> "I was far up on one of the top decks when I jumped. My bathrobe floated away, and it was icily cold."
>
> Robert Daniel, who jumped off the sinking *Titanic*

hypothermia: very low body heat that can lead to death

Going Down With the Ship

Many brave people stayed on the ship until the end. Some passengers dressed in their best clothes. They smoked their last cigars. Other passengers and crew did what they could to keep people safe and calm.

▲ *The* Titanic *tipped and flooded before it sank.*

▶ *The brave band members went down with the ship. They were heroes.*

The Band Played On

The ship's band played lively songs to keep people calm. Then the water began to rise around their feet. The band switched to sadder songs. They kept playing until they were washed away.

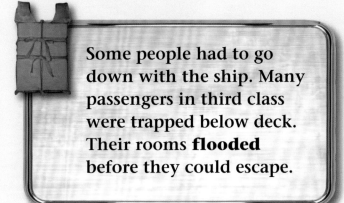

Some people had to go down with the ship. Many passengers in third class were trapped below deck. Their rooms **flooded** before they could escape.

 flooded: filled with water

The *Titanic* Sinks

Up in the Air

The *Titanic* sank deeper into the ocean. People watched in horror as the ship's **stern** tipped up into the air. Furniture and luggage and people came flying off the ship. Then the lights went out.

▲ *The stern of the* Titanic *tipped up into the air as the ship sank.*

Slipping Away

On April 15, at 2:20 a.m., the *Titanic* sank. The mighty ship split in two. Then it just slipped away. Only two and a half hours after hitting the iceberg, the unsinkable ship was gone.

"It was all over in an instant. The *Titanic*'s stern rose completely out of the water and went up ... into the air. Then ... slowly the *Titanic* slipped out of sight."

Titanic survivor Robert Daniel

stern: the back end of a ship

Into the Deep

More than 1,500 people died on that **tragic** day. Some were crushed as the ship fell apart. Others drowned in the deep water. Most people died of hypothermia. They froze to death waiting for the lifeboats to save them.

A rescue boat pulls up to a capsized lifeboat from the Titanic *to see if anyone is trapped underneath.*

"The partly filled lifeboats ... never came back. Why on Earth they never came back is a mystery."

Titanic survivor Jack Thayer

Plenty of Room

There were 20 lifeboats on the *Titanic*. Most of them had plenty of room. In fact, many boats were only half full. Only two lifeboats came back to look for survivors. Nine people were pulled from the icy water, but three of them soon died from the cold.

◀ The Titanic *sank into the dark ocean, leaving hundreds of people to die.*

tragic: very sad

The Rescue

The *Carpathia* headed for the sinking ship at full speed. Sadly, it arrived two hours after the *Titanic* had sunk. The *Carpathia*'s crew quickly pulled up the lifeboats. Then the crew helped the survivors climb to safety.

▲ *Survivors shared their sad stories on board the* Carpathia.

In Good Hands

The *Carpathia*'s crew took good care of the cold, hungry survivors. The crew gave people warm clothes and blankets. The crew fed the survivors hot meals and treated their **frostbite** and other wounds.

▼ *The crew of the* Carpathia *pulled up the lifeboats and saved the survivors.*

"We set foot on deck with very thankful hearts, grateful ...
to feel a solid ship beneath us once more."

Titanic survivor Lawrence Beesley, describing the rescue by the *Carpathia*

 frostbite: an injury caused by extreme cold

Survivors

More than 700 people escaped from the *Titanic*. Most of the survivors were women and children. They had boarded the lifeboats first. Men who survived were shamed. People said they should not have climbed into the lifeboats at all.

▲ *Michel and Edmond Navratil were two of the youngest survivors of the disaster.*

◄ *The "unsinkable" Molly Brown was a hero of the* Titanic.

Class Act

Most of the people who escaped came from first class. Only a few women and children from first class died in the **disaster**. The poor people in third class were not nearly as lucky.

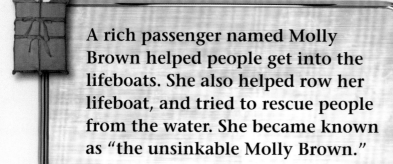

A rich passenger named Molly Brown helped people get into the lifeboats. She also helped row her lifeboat, and tried to rescue people from the water. She became known as "the unsinkable Molly Brown."

disaster: a sudden accident that causes great loss

Hoping and Praying

News of the disaster spread quickly. People around the world watched and waited. They hoped and prayed for survivors. Thousands of people met the *Carpathia* when it got to New York. People searched for their families and friends. Many never found them.

▲ *People around the world waited for news about the Titanic's victims.*

▲ *This crewman had bad frostbite on his feet.*

Moving On

Life was hard for survivors of the disaster. Many people had frostbite and other injuries. Immigrants moving to America lost everything they owned. Other people lost their whole family. All on board had seen horrors they would never forget.

After the disaster, ships pulled more than 300 dead bodies from the sea. The other **victims** of the *Titanic* were never found.

 victims: people who are hurt or killed in an accident

Finding the *Titanic*

Lost and Found

The *Titanic* was lost deep in the ocean. People searched for it for more than 70 years. In 1985, a scientist named Robert Ballard found the *Titanic* at last. His team used a small underwater craft called the *Argo* to track down the wreck.

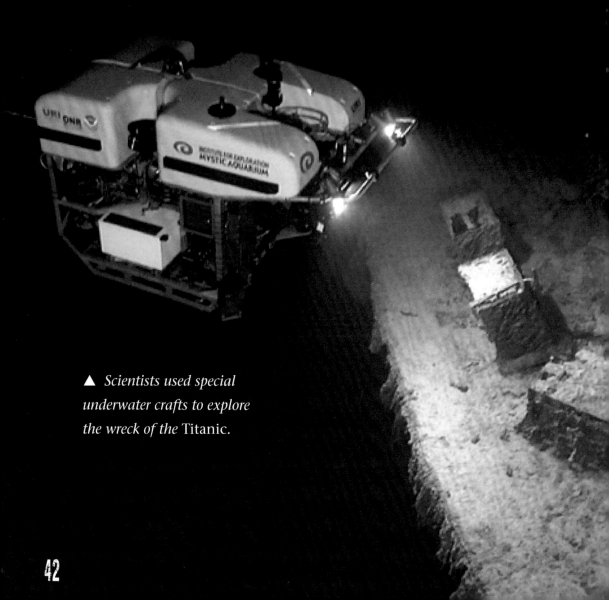

▲ *Scientists used special underwater crafts to explore the wreck of the* Titanic.

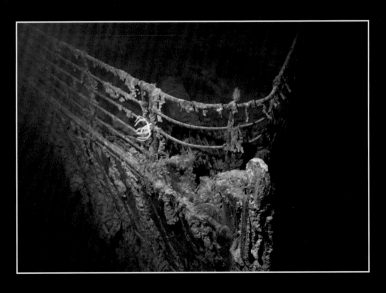

◀ *The bow (front) of the* Titanic *rusting at the bottom of the ocean.*

Following the Trail

The *Argo* moved along the dark ocean floor. It took pictures and sent them to people in a ship above. On September 1, the scientists saw pieces of the *Titanic*. They followed the trail of **debris**. The trail led the scientists to the ship.

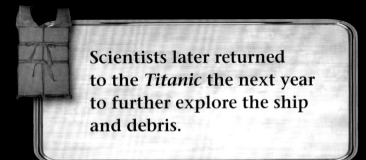

Scientists later returned to the *Titanic* the next year to further explore the ship and debris.

 debris: pieces of a wreck

The *Titanic* Today

Today, the rusty *Titanic* lies at the bottom of the Atlantic Ocean. The great ship is slowly **dissolving** into the sea floor. Scientists think the *Titanic* will be gone in 20 to 30 years.

▼ *Today, the wreck lies over 13,000 feet (3,962 m) down on the ocean floor.*

A Night to Remember

A hundred years have passed since the *Titanic* sank. The survivors have all died now, but their stories live on. Tales of the mighty *Titanic* and its tragic end keep the ship of dreams alive.

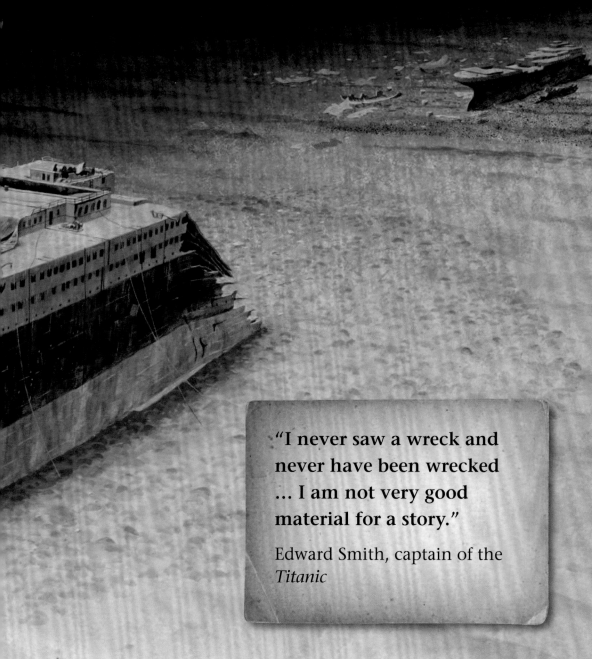

> "I never saw a wreck and never have been wrecked ... I am not very good material for a story."
>
> Edward Smith, captain of the *Titanic*

 dissolving: breaking down in water or other liquid

Books

Eyewitness Books: Titanic
by Simon Adams
(DK Publishing, 2009)

Finding the Titanic
by Robert D. Ballard
(Scholastic, 1993)

*Magic Tree House Research
Guide: Titanic*
by Mary Pope Osborne and
Will Osborne
(Random House, 2002)

*National Geographic Readers:
Titanic*
by Melissa Stewart
(National Geographic Society,
2012)

Movies

Ghosts of the Abyss
A non-fiction Disney film made
in 2003.

Secrets of the Titanic
A non-fiction film by National
Geographic.

Titanic
A popular 1997 fiction film
about the disaster.

Websites

National Geographic: Return to
Titanic.
*http://magma.national
geographic.com/ngexplorer/0411/
articles/mainarticle.html*

Encyclopedia Titanica.
*http://www.encyclopedia-
titanica.org/*

Glossary

abandon To leave a place and never go back to it

bridge An area where the captain and crew control a ship

collided Crashed into another object

debris Pieces of a wreck

disaster A sudden accident that causes great loss

dissolving Breaking down in water or other liquid

distress signals Radio signals that mean a ship is in danger

flooded Filled with water

frostbite An injury caused by extreme cold

hypothermia Very low body heat that can lead to death

icebergs Mountains of ice that float in the ocean

immigrants People who go to live in a new country

luxury Something fine or special that costs a lot of money

maiden voyage A ship's first trip

noble Being good and brave by helping others rather than yourself

ocean liner A large passenger ship with many comforts

stern The back end of a ship

strolled Walked slowly for pleasure

sturdy Solid and strong

tragic Very sad

victims People who are hurt or killed in an accident

Index

Entries in **bold** refer to pictures